Vera

Or, The Nihilists

Oscar Wilde

Alpha Editions

This edition published in 2024

ISBN : 9789362927354

Design and Setting By
Alpha Editions
www.alphaedis.com
Email - info@alphaedis.com

As per information held with us this book is in Public Domain.
This book is a reproduction of an important historical work. Alpha Editions uses the best technology to reproduce historical work in the same manner it was first published to preserve its original nature. Any marks or number seen are left intentionally to preserve its true form.

Contents

PERSONS IN THE PROLOGUE..- 1 -
PERSONS IN THE PLAY..- 2 -
PROLOGUE. ....- 3 -
ACT I. ....- 9 -
ACT II. ....- 21 -
ACT III. ....- 34 -
ACT IV. ....- 45 -

PERSONS IN THE PROLOGUE.

PETER SABOUROFF (an Innkeeper).
VERA SABOUROFF (his Daughter).
MICHAEL (a Peasant).
COLONEL KOTEMKIN.

                Scene, Russia. Time, 1795.

PERSONS IN THE PLAY.

IVAN THE CZAR.
PRINCE PAUL MARALOFFSKI (Prime Minister of Russia).
PRINCE PETROVITCH.
COUNT ROUVALOFF.
MARQUIS DE POIVRARD.
BARON RAFF.
GENERAL KOTEMKIN.
A PAGE.

Nihilists.

PETER TCHERNAVITCH, President of the Nihilists.
MICHAEL.
ALEXIS IVANACIEVITCH, known as a Student of Medicine.
PROFESSOR MARFA.
VERA SABOUROFF.

Soldiers, Conspirators, &c.

Scene, Moscow. Time, 1800.

PROLOGUE.

Scene.—*A Russian Inn.*

Large door opening on snowy landscape at back of stage.

Peter Sabouroff *and* Michael.

Peter (*warming his hands at a stove*). Has Vera not come back yet, Michael?

Mich. No, Father Peter, not yet; 'tis a good three miles to the post office, and she has to milk the cows besides, and that dun one is a rare plaguey creature for a wench to handle.

Peter. Why didn't you go with her, you young fool? she'll never love you unless you are always at her heels; women like to be bothered.

Mich. She says I bother her too much already, Father Peter, and I fear she'll never love me after all.

Peter. Tut, tut, boy, why shouldn't she? you're young and wouldn't be ill-favoured either, had God or thy mother given thee another face. Aren't you one of Prince Maraloffski's gamekeepers; and haven't you got a good grass farm, and the best cow in the village? What more does a girl want?

Mich. But Vera, Father Peter—

Peter. Vera, my lad, has got too many ideas; I don't think much of ideas myself; I've got on well enough in life without 'em; why shouldn't my children? There's Dmitri! could have stayed here and kept the inn; many a young lad would have jumped at the offer in these hard times; but he, scatter-brained featherhead of a boy, must needs go off to Moscow to study the law! What does he want knowing about the law! let a man do his duty, say I, and no one will trouble him.

Mich. Ay! but Father Peter, they say a good lawyer can break the law as often as he likes, and no one can say him nay.

Peter. That is about all they are good for; and there he stays, and has not written a line to us for four months now—a good son that, eh?

Mich. Come, come, Father Peter, Dmitri's letters must have gone astray—perhaps the new postman can't read; he looks stupid enough, and Dmitri, why, he was the best fellow in the village. Do you remember how he shot the bear at the barn in the great winter?

Peter. Ay, it was a good shot; I never did a better myself.

MICH. And as for dancing, he tired out three fiddlers Christmas come two years.

PETER. Ay, ay, he was a merry lad. It is the girl that has the seriousness—she goes about as solemn as a priest for days at a time.

MICH. Vera is always thinking of others.

PETER. There is her mistake, boy. Let God and our Little Father look to the world. It is none of my work to mend my neighbour's thatch. Why, last winter old Michael was frozen to death in his sleigh in the snowstorm, and his wife and children starved afterwards when the hard times came; but what business was it of mine? I didn't make the world. Let God and the Czar look to it. And then the blight came, and the black plague with it, and the priests couldn't bury the people fast enough, and they lay dead on the roads—men and women both. But what business was it of mine? I didn't make the world. Let God and the Czar look to it. Or two autumns ago, when the river overflowed on a sudden, and the children's school was carried away and drowned every girl and boy in it. I didn't make the world—let God and the Czar look to it.

MICH. But, Father Peter—

PETER. No, no, boy; no man could live if he took his neighbour's pack on his shoulders. (*Enter* VERA *in peasant's dress.*) Well, my girl, you've been long enough away—where is the letter?

VERA. There is none to-day, Father.

PETER. I knew it.

VERA. But there will be one to-morrow, Father.

PETER. Curse him, for an ungrateful son.

VERA. Oh, Father, don't say that; he must be sick.

PETER. Ay! sick of profligacy, perhaps.

VERA. How dare you say that of him, Father? You know that is not true.

PETER. Where does the money go, then? Michael, listen. I gave Dmitri half his mother's fortune to bring with him to pay the lawyer folk of Moscow. He has only written three times, and every time for more money. He got it, not at my wish, but at hers (*pointing to* VERA), and now for five months, close on six almost, we have heard nothing from him.

VERA. Father, he will come back.

PETER. Ay! the prodigals always return; but let him never darken my doors again.

VERA (*sitting down pensive*). Some evil has come on him; he must be dead! Oh! Michael, I am so wretched about Dmitri.

MICH. Will you never love any one but him, Vera?

VERA (*smiling*). I don't know; there is so much else to do in the world but love.

MICH. Nothing else worth doing, Vera.

PETER. What noise is that, Vera? (*A metallic clink is heard.*)

VERA (*rising and going to the door*). I don't know, Father; it is not like the cattle bells, or I would think Nicholas had come from the fair. Oh! Father! it is soldiers!—coming down the hill—there is one of them on horseback. How pretty they look! But there are some men with them with chains on! They must be robbers. Oh! don't let them in, Father; I couldn't look at them.

PETER. Men in chains! Why, we are in luck, my child! I heard this was to be the new road to Siberia, to bring the prisoners to the mines; but I didn't believe it. My fortune is made! Bustle, Vera, bustle! I'll die a rich man after all. There will be no lack of good customers now. An honest man should have the chance of making his living out of rascals now and then.

VERA. Are these men rascals, Father? What have they done?

PETER. I reckon they're some of those Nihilists the priest warns us against. Don't stand there idle, my girl.

VERA. I suppose, then, they are all wicked men.

(*Sound of soldiers outside; cry of "Halt!" enter Russian officer with a body of soldiers and eight men in chains, raggedly dressed; one of them on entering hurriedly puts his coat above his ears and hides his face; some soldiers guard the door, others sit down; the prisoners stand.*)

COLONEL. Innkeeper!

PETER. Yes, Colonel.

COLONEL (*pointing to Nihilists*). Give these men some bread and water.

PETER (*to himself*). I shan't make much out of that order.

COLONEL. As for myself, what have you got fit to eat?

PETER. Some good dried venison, your Excellency—and some rye whisky.

COLONEL. Nothing else?

PETER. Why, more whisky, your Excellency.

COLONEL. What clods these peasants are! You have a better room than this?

PETER. Yes, sir.

COLONEL. Bring me there. Sergeant, post your picket outside, and see that these scoundrels do not communicate with any one. No letter writing, you dogs, or you'll be flogged for it. Now for the venison. (*To* PETER *bowing before him.*) Get out of the way, you fool! Who is that girl? (*sees* VERA).

PETER. My daughter, your Highness.

COLONEL. Can she read and write?

PETER. Ay, that she can, sir.

COLONEL. Then she is a dangerous woman. No peasant should be allowed to do anything of the kind. Till your fields, store your harvests, pay your taxes, and obey your masters—that is your duty.

VERA. Who are our masters?

COLONEL. Young woman, these men are going to the mines for life for asking the same foolish question.

VERA. Then they have been unjustly condemned.

PETER. Vera, keep your tongue quiet. She is a foolish girl, sir, who talks too much.

COLONEL. Every woman does talk too much. Come, where is this venison? Count, I am waiting for you. How can you see anything in a girl with coarse hands? (*He passes with* PETER *and his aide-de-camp into an inner room.*)

VERA (*to one of the Nihilists*). Won't you sit down? you must be tired.

SERGEANT. Come now, young woman, no talking to my prisoners.

VERA. I shall speak to them. How much do you want?

SERGEANT. How much have you?

VERA. Will you let these men sit down if I give you this? (*Takes off her peasant's necklace.*) It is all I have; it was my mother's.

SERGEANT. Well, it looks pretty enough, and is heavy too. What do you want with these men?

VERA. They are hungry and tired. Let me go to them?

ONE OF THE SOLDIERS. Let the wench be, if she pays us.

SERGEANT. Well, have your way. If the Colonel sees you, you may have to come with us, my pretty one.

VERA (*advances to the Nihilists*). Sit down; you must be tired. (*Serves them food.*) What are you?

A PRISONER. Nihilists.

VERA. Who put you in chains?

PRISONER. Our Father the Czar.

VERA. Why?

PRISONER. For loving liberty too well.

VERA (*to prisoner who hides his face*). What did you want to do?

DMITRI. To give liberty to thirty millions of people enslaved to one man.

VERA (*startled at the voice*). What is your name?

DMITRI. I have no name.

VERA. Where are your friends?

DMITRI. I have no friends.

VERA. Let me see your face!

DMITRI. You will see nothing but suffering in it. They have tortured me.

VERA (*tears the cloak from his face*). Oh, God! Dmitri! my brother!

DMITRI. Hush! Vera; be calm. You must not let my father know; it would kill him. I thought I could free Russia. I heard men talk of Liberty one night in a café. I had never heard the word before. It seemed to be a new god they spoke of. I joined them. It was there all the money went. Five months ago they seized us. They found me printing the paper. I am going to the mines for life. I could not write. I thought it would be better to let you think I was dead; for they are bringing me to a living tomb.

VERA (*looking round*). You must escape, Dmitri. I will take your place.

DMITRI. Impossible! You can only revenge us.

VERA. I shall revenge you.

DMITRI. Listen! there is a house in Moscow—

SERGEANT. Prisoners, attention!—the Colonel is coming—young woman, your time is up.

(*Enter* COLONEL, AIDE-DE-CAMP *and* PETER.)

PETER. I hope your Highness is pleased with the venison. I shot it myself.

COLONEL. It had been better had you talked less about it. Sergeant, get ready. (*Gives purse to* PETER.) Here, you cheating rascal!

PETER. My fortune is made! long live your Highness. I hope your Highness will come often this way.

COLONEL. By Saint Nicholas, I hope not. It is too cold here for me. (*To* VERA.) Young girl, don't ask questions again about what does not concern you. I will not forget your face.

VERA. Nor I yours, or what you are doing.

COLONEL. You peasants are getting too saucy since you ceased to be serfs, and the knout is the best school for you to learn politics in. Sergeant, proceed.

(*The* COLONEL *turns and goes to top of stage. The prisoners pass out double file; as* DMITRI *passes* VERA *he lets a piece of paper fall on the ground; she puts her foot on it and remains immobile.*)

PETER (*who has been counting the money the* COLONEL *gave him*). Long life to your Highness. I will hope to see another batch soon. (*Suddenly catches sight of* DMITRI *as he is going out of the door, and screams and rushes up.*) Dmitri! Dmitri! my God! what brings you here? he is innocent, I tell you. I'll pay for him. Take your money (*flings money on the ground*), take all I have, give me my son. Villains! Villains! where are you bringing him?

COLONEL. To Siberia, old man.

PETER. No, no; take me instead.

COLONEL. He is a Nihilist.

PETER. You lie! you lie! He is innocent. (*The soldiers force him back with their guns and shut the door against him. He beats with his fists against it.*) Dmitri! Dmitri! a Nihilist! (*Falls down on floor.*)

VERA (*who has remained motionless, picks up paper now from under her feet and reads*). "99 Rue Tchernavaya, Moscow. To strangle whatever nature is in me; neither to love nor to be loved; neither to pity nor to be pitied; neither to marry nor to be given in marriage, till the end is come." My brother, I shall keep the oath. (*Kisses the paper.*) You shall be revenged!

(VERA *stands immobile, holding paper in her lifted hand.* PETER *is lying on the floor.* MICHAEL, *who has just come in, is bending over him.*)

END OF PROLOGUE.

ACT I.1

SCENE.—*99 Rue Tchernavaya, Moscow. A large garret lit by oil lamps hung from ceiling. Some masked men standing silent and apart from one another. A man in a scarlet mask is writing at a table. Door at back. Man in yellow with drawn sword at it. Knocks heard. Figures in cloaks and masks enter.*

Password. Per crucem ad lucem.

Answer. Per sanguinem ad libertatem.

(*Clock strikes.* CONSPIRATORS *form a semicircle in the middle of the stage.*)

2PRESIDENT. What is the word?

FIRST CONSP. Nabat.

PRES. The answer?

SECOND CONSP. Kalit.

PRES. What hour is it?

THIRD CONSP. The hour to suffer.

PRES. What day?

FOURTH CONSP. The day of oppression.

PRES. What year?

FIFTH CONSP. Since the Revolution of France, the ninth year.2

PRES. How many are we in number?

SIXTH CONSP. Ten, nine, and three.

PRES. The Galilæan had less to conquer the world; but what is our mission?

SEVENTH CONSP. To give freedom.

PRES. Our creed?

EIGHTH CONSP. To annihilate.

PRES. Our duty?

NINTH CONSP. To obey.

PRES. Brothers, the questions have been answered well. There are none but Nihilists present. Let us see each other's faces. (*The* CONSPIRATORS *unmask.*) Michael, recite the oath.

MICHAEL. To strangle whatever nature is in us; neither to love nor to be loved, neither to pity nor to be pitied, neither to marry nor to be given in marriage, till the end is come; to stab secretly by night; to drop poison in the glass; to set father against son, and husband against wife; without fear, without hope, without future, to suffer, to annihilate, to revenge.

PRES. Are we all agreed?

CONSPIRATORS. We are all agreed. (*They disperse in various directions about the stage.*)

PRES. 'Tis after the hour, Michael, and she is not yet here.

MICH. Would that she were! We can do little without her.

ALEXIS. She cannot have been seized, President? but the police are on her track, I know.

MICH. You always seem to know a good deal about the movements of the police in Moscow—too much for an honest conspirator.

PRES. If those dogs have caught her, 3the red flag of the people will float on a barricade in3 every street till we find her! It was foolish of her to go to the Grand Duke's ball. I told her so, but she said she wanted to see the Czar and all his cursed brood face to face once.

ALEXIS. Gone to the State ball?

MICH. I have no fear. She is as hard to capture as a she-wolf is, and twice as dangerous; besides, she is well disguised. But is there any news from the Palace to-night, President? What is that bloody4 despot doing now besides torturing his only son? Have any of you seen him? One hears strange stories about him. They say he loves the people; but a king's son never does that. You cannot breed them like that.

PRES. Since he came back from abroad a year ago his father has kept him in close prison in his palace.

MICH. An excellent training to make him a tyrant in his turn; but is there any news, I say?

PRES. A council is to be held to-morrow, at four o'clock, on some secret business the spies cannot find out.

MICH. A council in a king's palace is sure to be about some bloody work or other. But in what room is this council to be held?

PRES. (*reading from letter*). In the yellow tapestry room called after the Empress Catherine.

MICH. I care not for such long-sounding names. I would know where it is.

PRES. I cannot tell, Michael. I know more about the insides of prisons than of palaces.

MICH. (*speaking suddenly to* ALEXIS). Where is this room, Alexis?

ALEXIS. It is on the first floor, looking out on to the inner courtyard. But why do you ask, Michael?

MICH. Nothing, nothing, boy! I merely take a great interest in the Czar's life and movements, and I knew you could tell me all about the palace. Every poor student of medicine in Moscow knows all about king's houses. It is their duty, is it not?

ALEXIS (*aside*). Can Michael suspect me? There is something strange in his manner to-night. Why doesn't she come? The whole fire of revolution seems fallen into dull ashes when she is not here.

5MICH. Have you cured many patients lately, at your hospital, boy?

ALEX. There is one who lies sick to death I would fain cure, but cannot.

MICH. Ay, and who is that?

ALEX. Russia, our mother.

MICH. The curing of Russia is surgeon's business, and must be done by the knife. I like not your method of medicine.5

PRES. Professor, we have read the proofs of your last article; it is very good indeed.

MICH. What is it about, Professor?

PROFESSOR. The subject, my good brother, is assassination considered as a method of political reform.

MICH. I think little of pen and ink in revolutions. One dagger will do more than a hundred epigrams. Still, let us read this scholar's last production. Give it to me. I will read it myself.

PROF. Brother, you never mind your stops; let Alexis read it.

MICH. Ay! he is as tripping of speech as if he were some young aristocrat; but for my own part I care not for the stops so that the sense be plain.

ALEX. (*reading*). "The past has belonged to the tyrant, and he has defiled it; ours is the future, and we shall make it holy." Ay! let us make the future holy; let there be one revolution at least which is not bred in crime, nurtured in murder!

MICH. They have spoken to us by the sword, and by the sword we shall answer! You are too delicate for us, Alexis. There should be none here but men whose hands are rough with labour or red with blood.

PRES. Peace, Michael, peace! He is the bravest heart among us.

MICH. (*aside*). He will need to be brave to-night.

(*The sound of sleigh bells is heard outside.*)

VOICE (*outside*). Per crucem ad lucem.

Answer of man on guard. Per sanguinem ad libertatem.

MICH. Who is that?

VERA. God save the people!

PRES. Welcome, Vera, welcome! 6We have been sick at heart till we saw you; but now methinks the star of freedom has come to wake us from the night.6

VERA. 7It is night, indeed, brother! Night without moon or star!7 Russia is smitten to the heart! The man Ivan whom men call the Czar strikes now at our mother with a dagger deadlier than ever forged by tyranny against a people's life!

MICH. What has the tyrant8 done now?

VERA. To-morrow martial law is to be proclaimed in Russia.

OMNES. Martial law! We are lost! We are lost!

ALEX. Martial law! Impossible!

MICH. Fool, nothing is impossible in Russia but reform.

VERA. Ay, martial law. The last right to which the people clung has been taken from them. Without trial, without appeal, without accuser even, our brothers will be taken from their houses, shot in the streets like dogs, sent away to die in the snow, to starve in the dungeon, to rot in the mine. Do you know what martial law means? It means the strangling of a whole nation. 9The streets will be filled with soldiers night and day; there will be sentinels at every door.9 No man dare walk abroad now but the spy or the traitor. Cooped up in the dens we hide in, meeting by stealth, speaking with bated breath; what good can we do now for Russia?

PRES. We can suffer at least.

VERA. We have done that too much already. The hour is now come to annihilate and to revenge.

PRES. Up to this the people have borne everything.

VERA. Because they have understood nothing. But now we, the Nihilists, have given them the tree of knowledge to eat of and the day of silent suffering is over for Russia.

MICH. Martial law, Vera! This is fearful tidings you bring.

PRES. It is the death warrant of liberty in Russia.

VERA. Or the tocsin of10 revolution.

MICH. Are you sure it is true?

VERA. Here is the proclamation. I stole it myself at the ball to-night from a young fool, one of Prince Paul's secretaries, who had been given it to copy. It was that which made me so late.

(VERA *hands proclamation to* MICHAEL, *who reads it.*)

MICH. "To ensure the public safety—martial law. By order of the Czar, father of his people." The father of his people!

VERA. Ay! a father whose name shall not be hallowed, whose kingdom shall change to a republic, whose trespasses shall not be forgiven him, because he has robbed us of our daily bread; with whom is neither might, nor right, nor glory, now or for ever.

PRES. It must be about this that the council meet to-morrow. It has not yet been signed.

ALEX. It shall not be while I have a tongue to plead with.

MICH. Or while I have hands to smite with.

VERA. Martial law! O God, how easy it is for a king to kill his people by thousands, but we cannot rid ourselves of one crowned man in Europe! What is there of awful majesty in these men which makes the hand unsteady, the dagger treacherous, the pistol-shot harmless? Are they not men of like passions with ourselves, vulnerable to the same diseases, of flesh and blood not different from our own? What made Olgiati tremble at the supreme crisis of that Roman life, 11and Guido's nerve fail him when he should have been of iron and of steel? A plague, I say, on these fools of Naples, Berlin, and Spain!11 Methinks that if I stood face to face with one of the crowned men my eye would see more clearly, my aim be more sure, my whole body gain a strength and power that was not my own! Oh, to think what stands between us and freedom in Europe! a few old men, wrinkled, feeble, tottering dotards whom a boy could strangle for a ducat, or a woman stab in a night-time. And these are the things that keep us from democracy, that keep us from liberty. But now methinks the brood of men is dead and the dull earth grown sick of child-bearing, else would no crowned dog pollute God's air by living.

OMNES. Try us! Try us! Try us!

MICH. We shall try thee, too, some day, Vera.

VERA. I pray God thou mayest! Have I not strangled whatever nature is in me, and shall I not keep my oath?

MICH. (*to* PRESIDENT). Martial law, President! Come, there is no time to be lost. We have twelve hours yet before us till the council meet. 12Twelve hours! One can overthrow a dynasty in less time than that.12

PRES. 13Ay! or lose one's own head.13

(MICHAEL *and the* PRESIDENT *retire to one corner of the stage and sit whispering.* VERA *takes up the proclamation, and reads it to herself;* ALEXIS *watches and suddenly rushes up to her.*)

ALEX. Vera!

VERA. Alexis, you here! Foolish boy, have I not prayed you to stay away? All of us here are doomed to die before our time, fated to expiate by suffering whatever good we do; but you, with your 14bright boyish face,14 you are too young to die yet.

ALEX. One is never too young to die for one's country!

VERA. Why do you come here night after night?

ALEX. Because I love the people.

VERA. But your fellow-students must miss you. Are there no traitors among them? You know what spies there are in the University here. O Alexis, you must go! You see how desperate suffering has made us. There is no room here for a nature like yours. You must not come again.

ALEX. Why do you think so poorly of me? Why should I live while my brothers suffer?

VERA. You spake to me of your mother once. You said you loved her. Oh, think of her!

ALEX. I have no mother now but Russia, my life is hers to take or give away; but to-night I am here to see you. They tell me you are leaving for Novgorod to-morrow.

VERA. I must. They are getting faint-hearted there, and I would fan the flame of this revolution into such a blaze that the eyes of all kings in Europe shall be blinded. If martial law is passed they will need me all the more there. There is no limit, it seems, to the tyranny of one man; but there shall be a limit to the suffering of a whole people.

ALEX. God knows it, I am with you. But you must not go. 15The police are watching every train for you.15 When you are seized they have orders to place you without trial in the lowest dungeon of the palace.16 I know it—no matter how. 17Oh, think how without you the sun goes from our life, how the people will lose their leader and liberty her priestess.17 Vera, you must not go!

VERA. If you wish it, I will stay. I would live a little longer for freedom, a little longer for Russia.

ALEX. When you die then Russia is smitten indeed; when you die then I shall lose all hope—all.... Vera, this is fearful news you bring—martial law—it is too terrible. I knew it not, by my soul, I knew it not!

VERA. How could you have known it? It is too well laid a plot for that. This great White Czar, whose hands are red with the blood of the people he has murdered, whose soul is black with his iniquity, is the cleverest conspirator of us all. Oh, how could Russia bear two hearts like yours and his!

ALEX. Vera, the Emperor was not always like this. There was a time when he loved the people. It is that devil, whom God curse, Prince Paul Maraloffski who has brought him to this. To-morrow, I swear it, I shall plead for the people to the Emperor.

VERA. Plead to the Czar! Foolish boy, it is only those who are sentenced to death that ever see our Czar. Besides, what should he care for a voice that pleads for mercy? The cry of a strong nation in its agony has not moved that heart of stone.

ALEX. (*aside*). Yet shall I plead to him. They can but kill me.

PROF. Here are the proclamations, Vera. Do you think they will do?

VERA. I shall read them. 18How fair he looks?18 Methinks he never seemed so noble as to-night. Liberty is blessed in having such a lover.

ALEX. Well, President, what are you deep in?

MICH. We are thinking of the best way of killing bears. (*Whispers to* PRESIDENT *and leads him aside.*)

PROF. (*to* VERA). And the letters 19from our brothers at Paris and Berlin. What answer shall we send to them?19

VERA (*takes them mechanically*). Had I not strangled nature, sworn neither to love nor be loved, methinks20 I might have loved him. Oh, I am a fool, a traitor myself, a traitor myself! But why did he come amongst us with his bright21 young face, his heart aflame for liberty, his pure white soul? Why does he make me feel at times as if I would have him as my king, Republican though I be? Oh, fool, fool, fool! False to your oath! weak as water! Have done! Remember what you are—a Nihilist, a Nihilist!

PRES. (*to* MICHAEL). But you will be seized, Michael.

MICH. I think not. I will wear the uniform of the Imperial Guard, and the Colonel on duty is one of us. It is on the first floor, you remember; so I can take a long shot.

PRES. Shall I tell the brethren?

22MICH. Not a word, not a word! There is a traitor amongst us.

VERA. Come, are these the proclamations? Yes, they will do; yes, they will do. Send five hundred to Kiev and Odessa and Novgorod, five hundred to Warsaw, and have twice the number distributed among the Southern Provinces, though these dull Russian peasants care little for our proclamations, and less for our martyrdoms. When the blow is struck, it must be from the town, not from the country.

MICH. Ay, and by the sword not by the goose-quill.

VERA. Where are the letters from Poland?

PROF. Here.

VERA. Unhappy Poland! The eagles of Russia have fed on her heart. We must not forget our brothers there.22

PRES. Is this true, Michael?

MICH. Ay, I stake my life on it.

PRES. 23Let the doors be locked, then.23 Alexis Ivanacievitch entered on our roll of the brothers as a Student of the School of Medicine at Moscow. Why did you not tell us of this bloody scheme24 of martial law?

ALEX. I, President?

MICH. Ay, you! You knew it, none better. Such weapons as these are not forged in a day. Why did you not tell us of it? A week ago there had been time 25to lay the mine, to raise the barricade, to strike one blow at least for liberty.25 But now the hour is past. It is too late, 26it is too late!26 Why did you keep it a secret from us, I say?

ALEX. Now by the hand of freedom, Michael, my brother, you wrong me. I knew nothing of this hideous law. By my soul, my brothers, I knew not of it! How should I know?

MICH. Because you are a traitor! Where did you go when you left us the night of our last meeting here?

27ALEX. To mine own house, Michael.27

MICH. Liar! I was on your track. You left here an hour after midnight. Wrapped in a large cloak, you crossed the river in a boat a mile below the second bridge, and gave the ferryman a gold piece, you, the poor student of medicine! You doubled back twice, and hid in an archway so long that I had almost made up my mind to stab you at once, only that I am fond of hunting. So! you thought that you had baffled all pursuit, did you? Fool! I am a bloodhound that never loses the scent. I followed you from street to street. At last I saw you pass swiftly across the Place St. Isaac, whisper to the guards the secret password, enter the palace by a private door with your own key.

CONSPIRATORS. The palace!

VERA. Alexis!

MICH. I waited. All through the dreary watches of our long Russian night I waited, that I might kill you with your Judas hire still hot in your hand. But you never came out; you never left that palace at all. I saw the blood-red sun rise through the yellow fog over the murky town; I saw a new day of oppression dawn on Russia; but you never came out. So you pass nights in the palace, do you? You know the password for the guards! you have a key to a secret door. Oh, you are a spy—you are a spy! I never trusted you, 28with your soft white hands, your curled hair, your pretty graces.28 You have no mark of suffering about you; you cannot be of the people. You are a spy—29a spy—traitor.29

OMNES. Kill him! Kill him! (*draw their knives.*)

VERA (*rushing in front of* ALEXIS). Stand back, I say, Michael! Stand back all! 30Do not dare30 lay a hand upon him! He is the noblest heart amongst us.

OMNES. Kill him! Kill him! He is a spy!

VERA. Dare to lay a finger on him, and I leave you all to yourselves.

PRES. Vera, did you not hear what Michael said of him? He stayed all night in the Czar's palace. He has a password and a private key. What else should he be but a spy?

VERA. Bah! I do not believe Michael. It is a lie! It is31 a lie! Alexis, say it is a lie!

ALEX. It is true. Michael has told what he saw. I did pass that night in the Czar's palace. Michael has spoken the truth.

VERA. Stand back, I say; stand back! Alexis, I do not care. I trust you; you would not betray us; you would not sell the people for money. You are honest, true! Oh, say you are no spy!

ALEX. Spy? You know I am not. I am with you, my brothers, to the death.

MICH. Ay, to your own death.

ALEX. Vera, you32 know I am true.

VERA. I know it well.

PRES. Why are you here, traitor?

ALEX. Because I love the people.

MICH. Then you can be a martyr for them?

VERA. You must kill me first, Michael, before you lay a finger on him.

PRES. Michael, we dare not lose Vera. It is her whim to let this boy live. We can keep him here to-night. Up to this he has not betrayed us.

(*Tramp of soldiers outside, knocking at door.*)33

VOICE. Open in the name of the Emperor!

MICH. He *has* betrayed us. This is your doing, spy!

PRES. Come, Michael, come. We have no time to cut one another's throats while we have our own heads to save.

VOICE. Open in the name of the Emperor!

PRES. Brothers, be masked all of you. 34Michael, open the door. It is our only chance.34

(*Enter* GENERAL KOTEMKIN *and soldiers.*)

GEN. All honest citizens should be in their own houses at an hour before midnight, and not more than five people have a right to meet privately. Have you not noticed the proclamation, fellows?

MICH. Ay, you have spoiled every honest35 wall in Moscow with it.

VERA. Peace, Michael, peace. Nay, Sir, we knew it not. We are a company of strolling players travelling from Samara to Moscow to amuse His Imperial Majesty the Czar.

GEN. But I heard loud voices before I entered. What was that?

VERA. We were rehearsing a new tragedy.

GEN. Your answers are too *honest* to be true. Come, let me see who you are. Take off those players' masks. By St. Nicholas, my beauty, if your face matches your figure, you must be a choice morsel! Come, I say, pretty one; I would sooner see your face than those of all the others.

PRES. O God! if he sees it is Vera, we are all lost!

GEN. No coquetting, my girl. Come, unmask, I say, or I shall tell my guards to do it for you.

ALEX. Stand back, I say, General Kotemkin!

GEN. Who are you, fellow, that talk with such a tripping tongue to your betters? (ALEXIS *takes his mask off.*) His Imperial Highness the Czarevitch!

OMNES. The Czarevitch! 36It is all over!36

37PRES. He will give us up to the soldiers.37

MICH. (*to* VERA). Why did you not let me kill him? Come, we must fight to the death for it.

VERA. Peace! he will not betray us.

ALEX. A whim of mine, General! You know how my father keeps me from the world and imprisons me in the palace. I should really be bored to death if I could not get out at night in disguise sometimes, and have some romantic adventure in town. I fell in with these honest folks a few hours ago.

GEN. But, your Highness—

ALEX. Oh, they are excellent actors, I assure you. If you had come in ten minutes ago, you would have witnessed a most interesting scene.

GEN. Actors, are they, Prince?

ALEX. Ay, and very ambitious actors, too. They only care to play before kings.

GEN. I' faith, your Highness, I was in hopes I had made a good haul of Nihilists.38

ALEX. Nihilists in Moscow, General! with you as head of the police? Impossible!

GEN. So I always tell your Imperial father. But I heard at the council to-day that that woman Vera Sabouroff, the head of them, had been seen in this very city. The Emperor's face turned as white as the snow outside. I think I never saw such terror in any man before.

ALEX. She is a dangerous woman, then, this Vera Sabouroff?

GEN. The most dangerous in all Europe.

ALEX. Did you ever see her, General?

GEN. Why, five years ago, when I was a plain Colonel, I remember her, your Highness, a common waiting girl in an inn. If I had known then what she was going to turn out, I would have flogged her to death on the roadside. She is not a woman at all; she is a sort of devil! For the last eighteen months I have been hunting her, and caught sight of her once last September outside Odessa.

ALEX. How did you let her go, General?

GEN. I was by myself, and she shot one of my horses just as I was gaining on her. If I see her again I shan't miss my chance. The Emperor has put twenty thousand roubles on her head.

ALEX. I hope you will get it, General; but meanwhile you are frightening these honest people out of their wits, and disturbing the tragedy. Good night, General.

GEN. Yes; but I should like to see their faces, your Highness.

ALEX. No, General; you must not ask that; you know how these gipsies hate to be stared at.

GEN. Yes. But, your Highness—

ALEX. (*haughtily*). General, they are my friends, that is enough. And, General, not a word of this little adventure here, you understand. I shall rely on you.

GEN. I shall not forget, Prince. But shall we not see you back to the palace? The State ball is almost over and you are expected.

ALEX. I shall be there; but I shall return alone. Remember, not a word about my strolling players.

GEN. Or your pretty gipsy, eh, Prince? your pretty gipsy! I' faith, I should like to see her before I go; she has such fine eyes through her mask. Well, good night, your Highness; good night.

ALEX. Good night, General.

(*Exit* GENERAL *and the soldiers.*)

VERA (*throwing off her mask*). Saved! and by you!

ALEX. (*clasping her hand*). Brothers, you trust me now?

TABLEAU.

END OF ACT I.

ACT II.

SCENE.—*Council Chamber in the Emperor's Palace, hung with yellow tapestry. Table, with chair of State, set for the Czar; window behind, opening on to a balcony. As the scene progresses the light outside gets darker.*

Present.—PRINCE PAUL MARALOFFSKI, PRINCE PETROVITCH, COUNT ROUVALOFF, BARON RAFF, COUNT PETOUCHOF.

PRINCE PETRO. So our young scatter-brained Czarevitch has been forgiven at last, and is to take his seat here again.

PRINCE PAUL. Yes; if that is not meant as an extra punishment. For my own part, at least, I find these Cabinet Councils extremely exhausting.

PRINCE PETRO. Naturally; you are always speaking.

PRINCE PAUL. No; I think it must be that I have to listen sometimes.

COUNT R. Still, anything is better than being kept in a sort of prison, like he was—never allowed to go out into the world.

PRINCE PAUL. My dear Count, for romantic young people like he is, the world always looks best at a distance; and a prison where one's allowed to order one's own dinner is not at all a bad place. (*Enter the* CZAREVITCH. *The courtiers rise.*) Ah! good afternoon, Prince. Your Highness is looking a little pale to-day.

CZARE. (*slowly, after a pause*). I want change of air.

PRINCE PAUL (*smiling*). A most revolutionary sentiment! Your Imperial father would highly disapprove of any reforms with the thermometer in Russia.

CZARE. (*bitterly*). My Imperial father had kept me for six months in this dungeon of a palace. This morning he has me suddenly woke up to see some wretched Nihilists hung; it sickened me, the bloody butchery, though it was a noble thing to see how well these men can die.

PRINCE PAUL. When you are as old as I am, Prince, you will understand that there are few things easier than to live badly and to die well.

CZARE. Easy to die well! A lesson experience cannot have taught you, whatever you may know of a bad life.

PRINCE PAUL (*shrugging his shoulders*). Experience, the name men give to their mistakes. I never commit any.

CZARE. (*bitterly*). No; crimes are more in your line.

PRINCE PETRO. (*to the* CZAREVITCH). The Emperor was a good deal agitated about your late appearance at the ball last night, Prince.

1COUNT R. (*laughing*). I believe he thought the Nihilists had broken into the palace and carried you off.

BARON RAFF. If they had you would have missed a charming dance.1

PRINCE PAUL. And2 an excellent supper. Gringoire really excelled himself in his salad. Ah! you may laugh, Baron; but to make a good salad is a much more difficult thing than cooking accounts. To make a good salad is to be a brilliant diplomatist—the problem is so entirely the same in both cases. To know exactly how much oil one must put with one's vinegar.

BARON RAFF. A cook and a diplomatist! an excellent parallel. If I had a son who was a fool I'd make him one or the other.

PRINCE PAUL. I see your father did not hold the same opinion, Baron. But, believe me, you are wrong to run down cookery. For myself, the only immortality I desire is to invent a new sauce. I have never had time enough to think seriously about it, but I feel it is in me, I feel it is in me.

CZARE. You have certainly missed your *metier*,3 Prince Paul; the *cordon bleu* would have suited you much better than the Grand Cross of Honour. But you know you could never have worn your white apron well; you would have soiled it too soon, your hands are not clean enough.

PRINCE PAUL (*bowing*). Que voulez vous? I manage your father's business.

CZARE. (*bitterly*). You mismanage my father's business, you mean! Evil genius of his life that you are! before you came there was some love left in him. It is you who have embittered his nature, poured into his ear the poison of treacherous counsel, made him hated by the whole people, made him what he is—a tyrant!

(*The courtiers look significantly at each other.*)

PRINCE PAUL (*calmly*). I see your Highness does want change of air. But I have been an eldest son myself. (*Lights a cigarette.*) I know what it is when a father won't die to please one.

(*The* CZAREVITCH *goes to the top of the stage, and leans against the window, looking out.*)

PRINCE PETRO. (*to* BARON RAFF). Foolish boy! 4He will be sent into exile, or worse, if he is not careful.4

BARON RAFF. Yes.5 What a mistake it is to be sincere!

PRINCE PETRO. The only folly you have never committed, Baron.

BARON RAFF. One has only one head, you know, Prince.

PRINCE PAUL. My dear Baron, your head is the last thing any one would wish to take from you. (*Pulls out snuffbox and offers it to* PRINCE PETROVITCH.)

PRINCE PETRO. Thanks, Prince! Thanks!

PRINCE PAUL. Very delicate, isn't it? I get it direct from Paris. But under this vulgar Republic everything has degenerated over there. "Cotelettes à l'impériale" vanished, of course, with the Bourbon, and omelettes went out with the Orleanists. La belle France is entirely ruined, Prince, through bad morals and worse cookery. (*Enter the* MARQUIS DE POIVRARD.) Ah! Marquis. I trust Madame la Marquise is well.

MARQUIS DE P. You ought to know better than I do, Prince Paul; you see more *of* her.

PRINCE PAUL (*bowing*). Perhaps I see more *in* her, Marquis. Your wife is really a charming woman, so full of *esprit*, and so satirical too; she talks continually of you when we are together.

PRINCE PETRO. (*looking at the clock*). His Majesty is a little late to-day, is he not?

PRINCE PAUL. What has happened to you, my dear Petrovitch? you seem quite out of sorts. You haven't quarrelled with your cook, I hope? What a tragedy that would be for you; you would lose all your friends.

PRINCE PETRO. I fear I wouldn't be so fortunate as that. You forget I would still have my purse.6 But you are wrong for once; my chef and I are on excellent7 terms.

PRINCE PAUL. Then your creditors or Mademoiselle Vera Sabouroff have been writing to you? I find both of them such excellent correspondents. But really you needn't be alarmed. I find the most violent proclamations from the Executive Committee, as they call it, left all over my house. I never read them; they are so badly spelt as a rule.

PRINCE PETRO. Wrong again, Prince; the Nihilists leave me alone for some reason or other.

PRINCE PAUL (*aside*). Ah! true. I forgot. Indifference is the revenge the world takes on mediocrities.

PRINCE PETRO. I am bored with life,8 Prince. Since the opera season ended I have been a perpetual martyr to ennui.

PRINCE PAUL. The maladie du siècle! You want a new excitement, Prince. Let me see—you have been married twice already; suppose you try—falling in love, for once.

BARON R. Prince, I have been thinking a good deal lately—

PRINCE PAUL (*interrupting*). You surprise me very much, Baron.

BARON R. I cannot understand your nature.

PRINCE PAUL (*smiling*). If my nature had been made to suit your comprehension rather than my own requirements, I am afraid I would have made a very poor figure in the world.

COUNT R. There seems to be nothing in life about which you would not jest.

PRINCE PAUL. Ah! my dear Count, life is much too important a thing ever to talk seriously about it.

CZARE. (*coming back from the window*). I don't think Prince Paul's nature is such a mystery. He would stab his best friend for the sake of writing an epigram on his tombstone, or experiencing a new sensation.

PRINCE PAUL. Parbleu! I would sooner lose my best friend than my worst enemy. To have friends, you know, one need only be good-natured; but when a man has no enemy left there must be something mean about him.

CZARE. (*bitterly*). If to have enemies is a measure of greatness, then you must be a Colossus, indeed, Prince.

PRINCE PAUL. Yes, I know I'm the most hated man in Russia, except your father, 9except your father, of course,9 Prince. He doesn't seem to like it much, by the way, but I do, I assure you. (*Bitterly.*) I love to drive through the streets and see how the canaille scowl at me from every corner. It makes me feel I am a power in Russia; one man against a hundred millions! Besides, I have no ambition to be a popular hero, to be crowned with laurels one year and pelted with stones the next; I prefer dying peaceably in my own bed.

CZARE. And after death?

PRINCE PAUL (*shrugging his shoulders*). Heaven is a despotism. I shall be at home there.

CZARE. Do you never think of the people and their rights?

PRINCE PAUL. The people and their rights bore me. I am sick of both. In these modern days to be vulgar, illiterate, common and vicious, seems to give a man a marvellous infinity of rights that his honest fathers never dreamed of. Believe me, Prince, in good democracy every man should be an aristocrat;

but these people in Russia who seek to thrust us out are no better than the animals in one's preserves, and made to be shot at, most of them.

CZARE. (*excitedly*). If they are10 common, illiterate, vulgar, no better than the beasts of the field, who made them so?

(*Enter* AIDE-DE-CAMP.)

AIDE-DE-CAMP. His Imperial Majesty, the Emperor! (PRINCE PAUL *looks at the* CZAREVITCH, *and smiles.*)

(*Enter the* CZAR, *surrounded by his guard.*)

CZARE. (*rushing forward to meet him*). Sire!

CZAR (*nervous and frightened*). Don't come too near me, boy! Don't come too near me, I say! There is always something about an heir to a crown unwholesome to his father. Who is that man over there? I don't know him. What is he doing? Is he a conspirator? Have you searched him? Give him till to-morrow to confess, then hang him!—hang him!

PRINCE PAUL. Sire, you are anticipating history. This is Count Petouchof, your new ambassador to Berlin. He is come to kiss hands on his appointment.

CZAR. To kiss my hand? There is some plot in it. He wants to poison me. There, kiss my son's hand; it will do quite as well.

(PRINCE PAUL *signs to* COUNT PETOUCHOF *to leave the room. Exit* PETOUCHOF *and the guards.* CZAR *sinks down into his chair. The courtiers remain silent.*)

PRINCE PAUL (*approaching*). Sire! will your Majesty—

CZAR. What do you startle me like that for? No, I won't. (*Watches the courtiers nervously.*) Why are you clattering your sword, sir? (*To* COUNT ROUVALOFF.) Take it off, I shall have no man wear a sword in my presence (*looking at* CZAREVITCH), least of all my son. (*To* PRINCE PAUL.) You are not angry with me, Prince? You won't desert me, will you? Say you won't desert me. What do you want? You can have anything—anything.

PRINCE PAUL (*bowing very low*). Sire, 'tis enough for me to have your confidence. (*Aside.*) I was afraid he was going to revenge himself and give me another decoration.

CZAR (*returning to his chair*). Well, gentlemen.

MARQ. DE POIV. Sire, I have the honour to present to you a loyal address from your subjects in the Province of Archangel, expressing their horror at the last attempt on your Majesty's life.

PRINCE PAUL. The last attempt but two, you ought to have said, Marquis. Don't you see it is dated three weeks back?

CZAR. They are good people in the Province of Archangel—honest, loyal people. They love me very much—simple, loyal people; give them a new saint, it costs nothing. Well, Alexis (*turning to the* CZAREVITCH)—how many traitors were hung this morning?

CZARE. There were three men strangled, Sire.

CZAR. There should have been three11 thousand. I would to God that this people had but one neck that I might strangle them with one noose! Did they tell anything? whom did they implicate? what did they confess?

CZARE. Nothing, Sire.

CZAR. They should have been tortured then; why weren't they tortured? Must I always be fighting in the dark? Am I never to know from what root these traitors spring?

CZARE. What root should there be of discontent among the people but tyranny and injustice amongst their rulers?

CZAR. What did you say, boy? tyranny! tyranny! Am I a tyrant? I'm not. I love the people. I'm their father. I'm called so in every official proclamation. Have a care, boy; have a care. You don't seem to be cured yet of your foolish tongue. (*Goes over to* PRINCE PAUL, *and puts his hand on his shoulder.*) Prince Paul, tell me were there many people there this morning to see the Nihilists hung?

PRINCE PAUL. Hanging is of course a good deal less of a novelty in Russia now, Sire, than it was three or four years ago; and you know how easily the people get tired even of their best amusements. But the square and the tops of the houses were really quite crowded, were they not, Prince? (*To the* CZAREVITCH *who takes no notice.*)

CZAR. That's right; all loyal citizens should be there. It shows them what to look forward to. Did you arrest any one in the crowd?

PRINCE PAUL. Yes, Sire, a woman for cursing your name. (*The* CZAREVITCH *starts anxiously.*) She was the mother of the two criminals.

CZAR (*looking at* CZAREVITCH). She should have blessed me for having rid her of her children. Send her to prison.

CZARE. The prisons of Russia are too full already, Sire. There is no room in them for any more victims.

12CZAR. They don't die fast enough, then. You should put more of them into one cell at once. You don't keep them long enough in the mines. If you do they're sure to die; but you're all too merciful. I'm too merciful myself. Send her to Siberia.12 She is sure to die on the way. (*Enter an* AIDE-DE-CAMP.) Who's that? Who's that?

AIDE-DE-CAMP. A letter for his Imperial Majesty.

CZAR (*to* PRINCE PAUL). I won't open it. There may be something in it.

PRINCE PAUL. It would be a very disappointing letter, Sire, if there wasn't. (*Takes letter himself, and reads it.*)

PRINCE PETRO. (*to* COUNT ROUVALOFF). It must be some sad news. I know that smile too well.

PRINCE PAUL. From the Chief of the Police at Archangel, Sire. "The Governor of the province was shot this morning by a woman as he was entering the courtyard of his own house. The assassin has been seized."

CZAR. I never trusted the people of Archangel. It's a nest of Nihilists and conspirators. Take away their saints; they don't deserve them.

PRINCE PAUL. Your Highness would punish them more severely by giving them an extra one. Three governors shot in two months. (*Smiles to himself.*) Sire, permit me to recommend your loyal subject, the Marquis de Poivrard, as the new governor of your Province of Archangel.

MARQ. DE POIV. (*hurriedly*). Sire, I am unfit for this post.

PRINCE PAUL. Marquis, you are too modest. Believe me, there is no man in Russia I would sooner see Governor of Archangel than yourself. (*Whispers to* CZAR.)

CZAR. Quite right, Prince Paul; you are always right. See that the Marquis's letters are made out at once.

PRINCE PAUL. He can start to-night, Sire. I shall really miss you very much, Marquis. I always liked your taste in wines and wives extremely.

MARQ. DE POIV. (*to the* CZAR). Start to-night, Sire? (PRINCE PAUL *whispers to the* CZAR.)

CZAR. Yes, Marquis, to-night; it is better to go at once.

PRINCE PAUL. I shall see that Madame la Marquise is not too lonely while you are away; so you need not be alarmed for her.

COUNT R. (*to* PRINCE PETROVITCH). I should be more alarmed for myself.

CZAR. The Governor of Archangel shot in his own courtyard by a woman! I'm not safe here. I'm not safe anywhere, with that she devil of the revolution, Vera Sabouroff, here in Moscow. Prince Paul, is that woman still here?

PRINCE PAUL. They tell me she was at the Grand Duke's ball last night. I can hardly believe that; but she certainly had intended to leave for Novgorod to-day, Sire. The police were watching every train for her; but, for some reason or other, she did not go. Some traitor must have warned her. But I shall catch her yet. A chase after a beautiful woman is always exciting.

CZAR. You must hunt her down with bloodhounds, and when she is taken I shall hew her limb from limb. I shall stretch her on the rack till her pale white body is twisted and curled like paper in the fire.

PRINCE PAUL. Oh, we shall have another hunt immediately for her, Sire! Prince Alexis will assist us, I am sure.

CZARE. You never require any assistance to ruin a woman, Prince Paul.

CZAR. Vera, the Nihilist, in Moscow! O God,13 were it not better to die at once the dog's death they plot for me than to live as I live now! Never to sleep, or, if I do, to dream such horrid dreams that Hell itself were peace when matched with them. To trust none but those I have bought, to buy none worth trusting! To see a traitor in every smile, poison in every dish, a dagger in every hand! To lie awake at night, listening from hour to hour for the stealthy creeping of the murderer, for the laying of the damned mine! You are all spies! you are all spies! You worst of all—you, my own son! Which of you is it who hides these bloody proclamations under my own pillow, or at the table where I sit? Which of ye all is the Judas who betrays me? O God! O God! methinks there was a time once, in our war with England, when nothing could make me afraid. (*This with more calm and pathos.*) I have ridden into the crimson heart of war, and borne back an eagle which those wild islanders had taken from us. Men said I was brave then. My father gave me the Iron Cross of valour. Oh, could he see me now with this coward's livery ever in my cheek! (*Sinks into his chair.*) I never knew any love when I was a boy. I was ruled by terror myself, how else should I rule now? (*Starts up.*) But I will have revenge; I will have revenge. For every hour I have lain awake at night, waiting for the noose or the dagger, they shall pass years in Siberia, centuries in the mines! Ay! I shall have revenge.

CZARE. Father! have mercy on the people. Give them what they ask.

PRINCE PAUL. And begin, Sire, with your own head; they have a particular liking for that.

CZAR. The people! the people! A tiger which I have let loose upon myself; but I will fight with it to the death. 14I am done with half measures.14 I shall crush these Nihilists at a blow. There shall not be a man of them, ay, or a woman either, left alive in Russia. 15Am I Emperor for15 nothing, that a woman should hold me at bay? Vera Sabouroff shall be in my power, I swear it, before a week is ended, 16though I burn my whole city to find her.16 She shall be flogged by the knout, stifled in the fortress, strangled in the square!

CZARE. O God!

CZAR. For two years her hands have been clutching at my throat; for two years she has made my life a hell; but I shall have revenge. Martial law, Prince, martial law over the whole Empire; that will give me revenge. A good measure, Prince, eh? a good measure.

PRINCE PAUL. And an economical one too, Sire. It would carry off your surplus population in six months, and save you many expenses in courts of justice; they will not be needed now.

CZAR. Quite right. There are too many people in Russia, too much money spent on them, too much money in courts of justice. I'll shut them up.

CZARE. Sire, reflect before—

CZAR. When can you have the proclamations ready, Prince Paul?

PRINCE PAUL. They have been printed for the last six months, Sire. I knew you would need them.

CZAR. That's good! That's very good! Let us begin at once. Ah, Prince, if every king in Europe had a minister like you—

CZARE. There would be less kings in Europe than there are.

CZAR (*in frightened whisper, to* PRINCE PAUL). What does he mean? Do you trust him? His prison hasn't cured him yet. Shall I banish him? Shall I (*whispers*)...? The Emperor Paul did it. The Empress Catherine there17 (*points to picture on the wall*) did it. Why shouldn't I?

PRINCE PAUL. Your Majesty, there is no need for alarm. The Prince is a very ingenuous young man. He pretends to be devoted to the people, and lives in a palace; preaches socialism, and draws a salary that would support a province. He'll find out one day that the best cure for Republicanism is the Imperial crown, and will cut up the "bonnet rouge" of Democracy to make decorations for his Prime Minister.

CZAR. You are right. If he really loved the people, he could not be my son.

PRINCE PAUL. If he lived with the people for a fortnight, their bad dinners would soon cure him of his democracy. Shall we begin, Sire?

CZAR. At once. Read the proclamation. Gentlemen, be seated. Alexis, Alexis, I say, come and hear it! It will be good practice for you; you will be doing it yourself some day.

CZARE. I have heard too much of it already. (*Takes his seat at the table.* COUNT ROUVALOFF *whispers to him.*)

CZAR. What are you whispering about there, Count Rouvaloff?

COUNT R. I was giving his Royal Highness some good advice, your Majesty.

PRINCE PAUL. Count Rouvaloff is the typical spendthrift, Sire; he is always giving away what he needs most. (*Lays papers before the* CZAR.) I think, Sire, you will approve of this:—"Love of the people," "Father of his people," "Martial law," and the usual allusions to Providence in the last line. All it requires now is your Imperial Majesty's signature.

CZARE. Sire!

PRINCE PAUL (*hurriedly*). I promise your Majesty to crush every Nihilist in Russia in six months if you sign this proclamation; every Nihilist in Russia.

CZAR. Say that again! To crush every Nihilist in Russia; to crush this woman, their leader, who makes war upon me in my own city. Prince Paul Maraloffski, I create you Marechale of the whole Russian Empire to help you to carry out martial law.

CZAR. Give me the proclamation. I will sign it at once.

PRINCE PAUL (*points on paper*). Here, Sire.

CZARE. (*starts up and puts his hands on the paper*). Stay! I tell you, stay! The priests have taken heaven from the people, and you would take the earth away too.

PRINCE PAUL. We have no time, Prince, now. This boy will ruin everything. The pen, Sire.

CZARE. What! is it so small a thing to strangle a nation, to murder a kingdom, to wreck an empire? Who are we who dare lay this ban of terror on a people? Have we less vices than they have, that we bring them to the bar of judgment before us?

PRINCE PAUL. What a Communist the Prince is! He would have an equal distribution of sin as well as of property.

CZARE. Warmed by the same sun, nurtured by the same air, fashioned of flesh and blood like to our own, wherein are they different to us, save that they starve while we surfeit, that they toil while we idle, that they sicken while we poison, that they die while we strangle?

CZAR. How dare—?

CZARE. I dare all for the people; but you would rob them of common rights of common men.

CZAR. The people have no rights.

CZARE. Then they have great wrongs. Father, they have won your battles for you; from the pine forests of the Baltic to the palms of India they have ridden on victory's mighty wings in search of your glory! Boy as I am in years, I have seen wave after wave of living men sweep up the heights of battle to their death; ay, and snatch perilous conquest from the scales of war when the bloody crescent seemed to shake above our eagles.

CZAR (*somewhat moved*). Those men are dead. What have I to do with them?

CZARE. Nothing! The dead are safe; you18 cannot harm them now. They sleep their last long sleep. Some in Turkish waters, others by the windswept heights of Norway and the Dane! But these, the living, our brothers, what have you done for them? They asked you for bread, you gave them a stone. They sought for freedom, you scourged them with scorpions. You have sown the seeds of this revolution yourself!—

PRINCE PAUL. And are we not cutting down the harvest?

CZARE. Oh, my brothers! better far that ye had died in the iron hail and screaming shell of battle than to come back to such a doom as19 this! The beasts of the forests have their lairs, and the wild beasts their caverns, but the people of Russia, conquerors of the world, have not where to lay their heads.

PRINCE PAUL. They have the headsman's block.

CZARE. The headsman's block! Ay! you have killed their souls at your pleasure, you would kill their bodies now.

CZAR. Insolent boy! Have you forgotten who is Emperor of Russia?

CZARE. No! The people reign now, by the grace of God.20 You should have been their shepherd; you have fled away like the hireling, and let the wolves in upon them.

CZAR. Take him away! Take him away, Prince Paul!

CZARE. God hath given this people tongues to speak with; you would cut them out that they may be dumb in their agony, silent in their torture! But God hath given them hands to smite with, and they shall smite! Ay! from the sick and labouring womb of this unhappy land some revolution, like a bloody child, shall21 rise up and slay you.

CZAR (*leaping up*). Devil! Assassin! Why do you beard me thus to my face?

CZARE. Because I am a Nihilist! (*The ministers start to their feet; there is dead silence for a few minutes.*)

CZAR. A Nihilist! a Nihilist! Scorpion whom I have nurtured, traitor whom I have fondled, is this your bloody secret? Prince Paul Maraloffski, Marechale of the Russian Empire, arrest the Czarevitch!

MINISTERS. Arrest the Czarevitch!

CZAR. A Nihilist! If you have sown with them, you shall reap with them! If you have talked with them, you shall rot with them! If you have lived with them, with them you shall die!

PRINCE PETRO. Die!

CZAR. A plague on all sons, I say! There should be no more marriages in Russia when one can breed such vipers as you are! Arrest the Czarevitch, I say!

PRINCE PAUL. Czarevitch! by order of the Emperor, I demand your sword. (CZAREVITCH *gives up sword;* PRINCE PAUL *places it on the table.*) Foolish boy! you are not made for a conspirator; you have not learned to hold your tongue. Heroics are out of place in a palace.

CZAR (*sinks into his chair with his eyes fixed on the* CZAREVITCH). O God!

CZARE. If I am to die for the people, I am ready; one Nihilist more or less in Russia, what does that matter?

PRINCE PAUL (*aside*). A good deal I should say to the one Nihilist.

CZARE. The mighty brotherhood to which I belong has a thousand such as I am, ten thousand better still! (*The* CZAR *starts in his seat.*) The star of freedom is risen already, and far off I hear the mighty wave democracy break on these cursed shores.

PRINCE PAUL (*to* PRINCE PETROVITCH). In that case you and I had better learn how to swim.

CZARE. Father, Emperor, Imperial Master, I plead not for my own life, but for the lives of my brothers, the people.

PRINCE PAUL (*bitterly*). Your brothers, the people, Prince, are not content with their own lives, they always want to take their neighbour's too.

CZAR (*standing up*). I am sick of being afraid. I have done with terror now. From this day I proclaim war against the people—war to their annihilation. As they have dealt with me, so shall I deal with them. I shall grind them to powder, and strew their dust upon the air. There shall be a spy in every man's house, a traitor on every hearth, a hangman in every village, a gibbet in every square. Plague, leprosy, or fever shall be less deadly than my wrath; I will make every frontier a grave-yard, every province a lazar-house, and cure the sick by the sword. I shall have peace in Russia, though it be the peace of the dead. Who said I was a coward? Who said I was afraid? See, thus shall I crush this people beneath my feet! (*Takes up sword of* CZAREVITCH *off table and tramples on it.*)

CZARE. Father, beware, the sword you tread on may turn and wound you. The people suffer long, but vengeance comes at last, vengeance with red hands and bloody purpose.

PRINCE PAUL. Bah! the people are bad shots; they always miss one.

CZARE. There are times when the people are instruments of God.

CZAR. Ay! and when kings are God's scourges for the people. Oh, my own son, in my own house! My own flesh and blood against me! Take him away! Take him away! Bring in my guards. (*Enter the Imperial Guard.* CZAR *points to* CZAREVITCH, *who stands alone at the side of the stage.*) To the blackest prison in Moscow! Let me never see his face again. (CZAREVITCH *is being led out.*) No, no, leave him! I don't trust guards. They are all Nihilists! They would let him escape and he would kill me, kill me! No, I'll bring him to prison myself, you and I (*to* PRINCE PAUL). I trust you, you have no mercy. I shall have no mercy. Oh, my own son against me! How hot it is! The air stifles me! I feel as if I were going to faint, as if something were at my throat. Open the windows, I say! Out of my sight! Out of my sight! I can't bear his eyes. Wait, wait for me. (*Throws window open and goes out on balcony.*)

PRINCE PAUL (*looking at his watch*). The dinner is sure to be spoiled. How annoying politics are and eldest sons!

VOICE (*outside, in the street*). God save the people! (CZAR *is shot, and staggers back into the room.*)

CZARE. (*breaking from the guards, and rushing over*). Father!

CZAR. Murderer! Murderer! You did it! Murderer! (*Dies.*)

TABLEAU.

END OF ACT II.

ACT III.

Same scene and business as Act I. Man in yellow dress, with drawn sword, at the door.

Password outside. Væ tyrannis.

Answer. Væ victis (*repeated three times*).

(*Enter* CONSPIRATORS, *who form a semicircle, masked and cloaked.*)

PRESIDENT. What hour is it?

FIRST CONSP. The hour to strike.

PRES. What day?

SECOND CONSP. The day of Marat.1

PRES. In what month?

SECOND CONSP. The month of liberty.

PRES. What is our duty?

FOURTH CONSP. To obey.

PRES. Our creed?

FIFTH CONSP. Parbleu, Mons. le President, I never knew you had one.

CONSPS. A spy! A spy! Unmask! Unmask! A spy!

PRES. 2Let the doors be shut. There are others but Nihilists present.2

CONSPS. Unmask! Unmask! 3Kill him! kill him!3 (*Masked* CONSPIRATOR *unmasks.*) Prince Paul!

VERA. Devil! Who lured you into the lion's den?

CONSPS. Kill him! kill him!4

PRINCE PAUL. En vérité, Messieurs, you are not over-hospitable in your welcome.

VERA. Welcome! What welcome should we give you but the dagger or the noose?

PRINCE PAUL. I had no idea, really, that the Nihilists were so exclusive. Let me assure you that if I had not always had an *entrée* to the very best society, and the very worst conspiracies, I could never have been Prime Minister in Russia.

VERA. The tiger cannot change its nature, nor the snake lose its venom; but are you turned a lover of the people?

PRINCE PAUL. Mon Dieu, non, Mademoiselle! I would much sooner talk scandal in a drawing-room than treason in a cellar. Besides, I hate the common mob, who smell of garlic, smoke bad tobacco, get up early, and dine off one dish.

PRES. What have you to gain, then, by a revolution?

PRINCE PAUL. Mon ami, I have nothing left to lose. That scatter-brained boy, this new Czar, has banished me.

VERA. To Siberia?

PRINCE PAUL. No, to Paris. He has confiscated my estates, robbed me of my office and my cook. I have nothing left but my decorations. I am here for revenge.5

PRES. Then you have a right to be one of us. 5We also meet daily for revenge.5

PRINCE PAUL. You want money, of course. No one ever joins a conspiracy who has any. Here. (*Throws money on table.*) You have so many spies that I should think you want information. Well, you will find me the best informed man in Russia on the abuses of our Government. I made them nearly all myself.

VERA. President, I don't trust this man. He has done us too much harm in Russia to let him go in safety.

PRINCE PAUL. Believe me, Mademoiselle, you are wrong; I will be a most valuable addition to your circle; as for you, gentlemen, if I had not thought that you would be useful to me I shouldn't have risked my neck among you, or dined an hour earlier than usual so as to be in time.

PRES. Ay, if he had wanted to spy on us, Vera, he wouldn't have come himself.

PRINCE PAUL (*aside*). No; I should have sent my best friend.

PRES. Besides, Vera, he is just the man to give us the information we want about some business we have in hand to-night.

VERA. Be it so if you wish it.

PRES. Brothers, is it your will that Prince Paul Maraloffski be admitted, and take the oath of the Nihilist?

CONSPS. It is! it is!

PRES. (*holding out dagger and a paper*). Prince Paul, the dagger or the oath?

PRINCE PAUL (*smiles sardonically*). I would sooner annihilate than be annihilated. (*Takes paper.*)

PRES. Remember: 6Betray us, and as long as the earth holds poison or steel, as long as men can strike or woman betray, you shall not escape vengeance.6 The Nihilists never forget their friends, or forgive their enemies.

PRINCE PAUL. Really? I did not think you were so civilized.

VERA (*pacing up and down*). Why is he not here? He will not keep the crown. I know him well.

PRES. Sign. (PRINCE PAUL *signs.*) You said you thought we had no creed. You were wrong. Read it!

VERA. This is a dangerous thing, President. What can we do with this man?

PRES. We can use him.

VERA. And afterwards?

PRES. (*shrugging his shoulders*). Strangle him.

PRINCE PAUL (*reading*). "The rights of humanity!" In the old times men carried out their rights for themselves as they lived, but nowadays every baby seems born with a social manifesto in its mouth much bigger than itself.7 "Nature is not a temple, but a workshop: we demand the right to labour." Ah, I shall surrender my own rights in that respect.

VERA (*pacing up and down behind*). Oh, will he never come? will he never come?

PRINCE PAUL. "The family as subversive of true socialistic and communal unity is to be annihilated." Yes, President, I agree completely with Article 5. A family is a terrible incumbrance, especially when one is not married. (*Three knocks at the door.*)

VERA. Alexis at last!

Password. Væ tyrannis!

Answer. Væ victis!

(*Enter* MICHAEL STROGANOFF.)

PRES.8 Michael, the regicide! Brothers, let us do honour to a man who has killed a king.

9VERA (*aside*). Oh, he will come yet.9

PRES. Michael, you have saved Russia.

MICH. Ay, Russia was free for a moment 10when the tyrant fell, but the sun of liberty has set again like that false dawn which cheats our eyes in autumn.

PRES. The dread night of tyranny is not yet past for Russia.

MICH. (*clutching his knife*).10 One more blow, and the end is come indeed.

VERA (*aside*). One more blow! What does he mean? Oh, impossible! but why is he not with us? Alexis! Alexis! why are you not here?

PRES. But how did you escape, Michael? They said you had been seized.

MICH. I was dressed in the uniform of the Imperial Guard. The Colonel on duty was a brother, and gave me the password. I drove through the troops in safety with it, and, thanks to my good horse, reached the walls before the gates were closed.

PRES. What a chance his coming out on the balcony was!

MICH. A chance? There is no such thing as chance. It was God's finger led him there.

PRES. And where have you been these three days?

MICH. Hiding in the house of the priest Nicholas at the cross-roads.

PRES. Nicholas is an honest man.

MICH. Ay, honest enough for a priest. I am here now for vengeance on a traitor!

VERA (*aside*). O God, will he never come? Alexis! why are you not here? You cannot have turned traitor!

MICH. (*seeing* PRINCE PAUL). Prince Paul Maraloffski here! By St. George, a lucky capture! This must have been Vera's doing. She is the only one who could have lured that serpent into the trap.

PRES. Prince Paul has just taken the oath.

VERA. Alexis, the Czar, has banished him from Russia.

MICH. Bah! A blind to cheat us. We will keep Prince Paul here, 11and find some office for him in our reign of terror.11 He is well accustomed by this time to bloody work.

PRINCE PAUL (*approaching* MICHAEL). That was a long shot of yours, mon camarade.

MICH. I have had a good deal of practice shooting, since I have been a boy, off your Highness's wild boars.

PRINCE PAUL. Are my gamekeepers like moles, then, always asleep?

MICH. No, Prince. I am one of them; but, like you, I am fond of robbing what I am put to watch.

PRES. This must be a new atmosphere for you, Prince Paul. We speak the truth to one another here.

PRINCE PAUL. How misleading you must find it. You have an odd medley here, President—a little rococo, I am afraid.

PRES. You recognise a good many friends, I dare say?

PRINCE PAUL. Yes, there is always more brass than brains in an aristocracy.

PRES. But you are here yourself?

PRINCE PAUL. I? As I cannot be Prime Minister, I must be a Nihilist. There is no alternative.

VERA. O God, will he never come? The hand is on the stroke of the hour. Will he never come?

MICH. (*aside*). President, you know what we have to do? 'Tis but a sorry hunter who leaves the wolf cub alive to avenge his father. How are we to get at this boy? It must be to-night. To-morrow he will be throwing some sop of reform to the people, and it will be too late for a Republic.

PRINCE PAUL. You are quite right. Good kings are the enemies of Democracy, and when he has begun by banishing me you may be sure he intends to be a patriot.

MICH. I am sick of patriot kings; 12what Russia needs is a Republic.12

PRINCE PAUL. Messieurs, I have brought you two documents which I think will interest you—the proclamation this young Czar intends publishing to-morrow, and a plan of the Winter Palace, where he sleeps to-night. (*Hands paper.*)

VERA. 13I dare not ask them what they are plotting about.13 Oh, why is Alexis not here?

PRES. Prince, this is most valuable information. Michael, you were right. If it is not to-night it will be too late. Read that.

MICH. Ah! A loaf of bread flung to a starving nation. 14A lie to cheat the people.14 (*Tears it up.*) It must be to-night. I do not believe in him. Would he have kept his crown had he loved the people? But how are we to get at him?

PRINCE PAUL. The key of the private door in the street. (*Hands key.*)

PRES. Prince, we are in your debt.

PRINCE PAUL (*smiling*). The normal condition of the Nihilists.

MICH. Ay, but we are paying our debts off with interest now. Two Emperors in one week. That will make the balance straight. We would have thrown in a Prime Minister if you had not come.

PRINCE PAUL. Ah, I am sorry you told me. It robs my visit of all its picturesqueness and adventure. I thought I was perilling my head by coming here, and you tell me I have saved it. One is sure to be disappointed if one tries to get romance out of modern life.

MICH. It is not so romantic a thing to lose one's head, Prince Paul.

PRINCE PAUL. No, but it must often be very dull to keep it. Don't you find that sometimes? (*Clock strikes six.*)

VERA (*sinking into a seat*). Oh, it is past the hour! It is past the hour!

MICH. (*to* PRESIDENT). Remember to-morrow will be too late.

PRES. Brothers, it is full time. Which of us is absent?

CONSPS. Alexis! Alexis!

PRES. Michael, read Rule 7.

MICH. "When any brother shall have disobeyed a summons to be present, the President shall enquire if there is anything alleged against him."

PRES. Is there anything against our brother Alexis?

CONSPS. He wears a crown! He wears a crown!

PRES. Michael, read Article 7 of the Code of Revolution.

MICH. "Between the Nihilists and all men who wear crowns above their fellows, there is war to the death."

PRES. Brothers, what say you? Is Alexis, the Czar, guilty or not?

OMNES. He is guilty!

PRES. What shall the penalty be?

OMNES. Death!

PRES. Let the lots be prepared; it shall be to-night.

PRINCE PAUL. Ah, this is really interesting! I was getting afraid conspiracies were as dull as courts are.

PROF. MARFA. My forte is more in writing pamphlets than in taking shots. Still a regicide has always a place in history.

MICH. If your pistol is as harmless as your pen, this young tyrant will have a long life.

PRINCE PAUL. You ought to remember, too, Professor, that if you were seized, as you probably would be, and hung, as you certainly would be, there would be nobody left to read your own articles.

PRES. Brothers, are you ready?

VERA (*starting up*). Not yet! Not yet! I have a word to say.

MICH. (*aside*). 15Plague take her! I knew it would come to this.15

VERA. This boy has been our brother. Night after night he has perilled his own life to come here. 16Night after night, when every street was filled with spies, every house with traitors.16 Delicately nurtured like a king's son, he has dwelt among us.

PRES. Ay! under a false name. 17He lied to us at the beginning. He lies to us now at the end.17

VERA. I swear he is true. There is not a man here who does not owe him his life a thousand times. When the bloodhounds were on us that night, who saved us 18from arrest, torture, flogging, death,18 but he ye seek to kill?—

MICH. To kill all tyrants is our mission!

VERA. He is no tyrant. I know him well! He loves the people.

PRES. We know him too; he is a traitor.

VERA. A traitor! Three days ago he could have betrayed every man of you here, 19and the gibbet would have been your doom.19 He gave you all your lives once. Give him a little time—a week, a month, a few days; but not now!—O God,20 not now!

CONSPS. (*brandishing daggers*). To-night! to-night! to-night!

VERA. Peace, you gorged adders; peace!

MICH. What, are we not here to annihilate? shall we not keep our oath?

VERA. Your oath! your oath! 21Greedy that you are of gain, every man's hand lusting for his neighbour's pelf, every heart set on pillage and rapine;21 who, of ye all, if the crown were set on his head, would give an empire up for the mob to scramble for? The people are not yet fit for a Republic in Russia.

PRES. Every nation is fit for a Republic.

MICH. The man is a tyrant.

VERA. A tyrant! Hath he not dismissed his evil counsellors. That ill-omened raven of his father's life hath had his wings clipped and his claws pared, and comes to us croaking for revenge. Oh, have mercy on him!22 Give him a week to live!

PRES. Vera pleading for a king!

VERA (*proudly*). I plead not for a king, but for a brother.

MICH. For a traitor to his oath, for a coward who should have flung the purple back to the fools that gave it to him. No, Vera, no. The brood of men is not dead yet, nor the dull earth grown sick of child-bearing. No crowned man in Russia shall pollute God's air by living.

PRES. You bade us try you once; we have tried you, and you are found wanting.

MICH. Vera, I am not blind; I know your secret. You love this boy, this young prince with his pretty face, his curled hair, his soft white hands. Fool that you are, dupe of a lying tongue, do you know what he would have done to you, this boy you think loved you? He would have made you his mistress, used your body at his pleasure, thrown you away when he was wearied of you; you, the priestess of liberty, the flame of Revolution, the torch of democracy.

VERA. What he would have done to me matters little. To the people, at least, he will be true. He loves the people—at least, he loves liberty.

PRES. So he would play the citizen-king, would he, while we starve? 23Would flatter us with sweet speeches, would cheat us with promises like his father, would lie to us as his whole race have lied.23

MICH. And you whose very name made every despot tremble for his life, you, Vera Sabouroff, you would betray liberty for a lover and the people for a paramour!

CONSPS. 24Traitress! Draw the lots; draw the lots!24

VERA. In thy throat thou liest, Michael! I love him not. He loves me not.

MICH. You love him not? Shall he not die then?

VERA (*with an effort, clenching her hands*). Ay, it is right that he should die. He hath broken his oath. 25There should be no crowned man in Europe. Have I not sworn it? To be strong our new Republic should be drunk with the blood of kings. He hath broken his oath. As the father died so let the son die too.25 Yet not to-night, not to-night. Russia, that hath borne her centuries of wrong, can wait a week for liberty. Give him a week.

PRES. We will have none of you! Begone from us to this boy you love.

MICH. Though I find him in your arms I shall kill him.

CONSPS. To-night! To-night! To-night!

MICH. (*holding up his hand*). A moment! I have something to say. (*Approaches* VERA; *speaks very slowly*.) Vera Sabouroff, have you forgotten your brother?

(*Pauses to see effect;* VERA *starts.*) Have you forgotten that young face, pale with famine; those young limbs twisted with torture; the iron chains they made him walk in? What week of liberty did they give him? What pity did they show him for a day? (VERA *falls in a chair.*) Oh! you could talk glibly enough then of vengeance, glibly enough of liberty. When you said you would come to Moscow, your old father caught you by the knees and begged you not to leave him childless and alone.26 I seem to hear his cries still ringing in my ears, but you were as deaf to him as the rocks on the roadside; as chill and cold as the snow on the hill. You left your father that night, and three weeks after he died of a broken heart. You wrote me to follow you here. I did so; first because I loved you; but you soon cured me of that; whatever gentle feeling, whatever pity, whatever humanity, was in my heart you withered up and destroyed, as the canker worm eats the corn, and the plague kills the child. You bade me cast out love from my breast as a vile thing, you turned my hand to iron, and my heart to stone; you told me to live for freedom and for revenge. I have done so; but you, what have you done?

VERA. Let the lots be drawn! (CONSPIRATORS *applaud.*)

PRINCE PAUL (*aside*). Ah, the Grand Duke will come to the throne sooner than he expected. He is sure to make a good king under my guidance. He is so cruel to animals, and never keeps his word.

MICH. Now you are yourself at last, Vera.

VERA (*standing motionless in the middle*). The lots, I say, the lots! I am no woman now. My blood seems turned to gall; my heart is as cold as steel is; my hand shall be more deadly. From the desert and the tomb the voice of my prisoned brother cries aloud, and bids me strike one blow for liberty. The lots, I say, the lots!

PRES. Are you ready. Michael, you have the right to draw first; you are a Regicide.

VERA. O God, into my hands! Into my hands! (*They draw the lots from a bowl surmounted by a skull.*)

PRES. Open your lots.

VERA (*opening her lot*). The lot is mine! see the bloody sign upon it! Dmitri, my brother, you shall have your revenge now.

PRES. Vera Sabouroff, you are chosen to be a regicide. God has been good to you. The dagger or the poison? (*Offers her dagger and vial.*)

VERA. I can trust my hand better with the dagger; it never fails. (*Take dagger.*) I shall stab him to the heart, as he has stabbed me. Traitor, to leave us for a ribbon, a gaud, a bauble, to lie to me every day he came here, to forget us in an hour. 27Michael was right, he loved me not, nor the people either.27 Methinks that if I was a mother and bore a man-child I would poison my breast to him, lest he might grow to a traitor or to a king. (PRINCE PAUL *whispers to the* PRESIDENT.)

PRES. Ay, Prince Paul, that is the best way. Vera, the Czar28 sleeps to-night in his own room in the north wing of the palace. Here is the key of the private door in the street. The passwords of the guards will be given to you. His own servants will be drugged. You will find him alone.

VERA. It is well. I shall not fail.

PRES. We will wait outside in the Place St. Isaac, under the window. As the clock strikes twelve from the tower of St. Nicholas you will give us the sign that the dog is dead.

VERA. And what shall the sign be?

PRES. You are to throw us out the bloody dagger.

MICH. Dripping with the traitor's life.

PRES. Else we shall know that you have been seized, and we will burst our way in, drag you from his guards.

MICH. And kill him in the midst of them.

PRES. Michael, you will head us?

MICH. Ay, I shall head you. See that your hand fails not, Vera Sabouroff.

29VERA. Fool, is it so hard a thing to kill one's enemy.29

PRINCE PAUL (*aside*). This is the ninth conspiracy I have been in in Russia. They always end in a "voyage en Siberie" for my friends and a new decoration for myself.

MICH. It is your last conspiracy, Prince.

PRES. At twelve o'clock, the bloody dagger.

VERA. Ay, red with the blood of that false heart. I shall not forget it. (*Standing in the middle of the stage.*) 30To strangle whatever nature is in me, neither to love nor to be loved, neither to pity nor to be pitied. Ay! it is an oath, an oath. Methinks the spirit of Charlotte Corday has entered my soul now. I shall carve my name on the world, and be ranked among the great heroines. Ay! the spirit of Charlotte Corday beats in each petty vein, and nerves my woman's hand to strike, as I have nerved my woman's heart to hate. Though he laughs in his dreams, I shall not falter. Though he sleep peacefully I shall not miss my blow.30 Be glad, my brother, in your stifled cell; be glad and laugh to-night. To-night this new-fledged Czar shall post with bloody feet to

Hell, and greet his father there! 31This Czar! O traitor, liar, false to his oath, false to me! To play the patriot amongst us, and now to wear a crown; to sell us, like Judas, for thirty silver pieces, to betray us with a kiss!31 (*With more passion.*) O Liberty, O mighty mother of eternal time, thy robe is purple with the blood of those who have died for thee! Thy throne is the Calvary of the people, thy crown the crown of thorns. O crucified mother, the despot has driven a nail through thy right hand, and the tyrant through thy left! Thy feet are pierced with their iron. When thou wert athirst thou calledst on the priests for water, and they gave thee bitter drink. They thrust a sword into thy side. They mocked thee in thine agony of age on age. 32Here, on thy altar, O Liberty, do I dedicate myself to thy service; do with me as thou wilt!32 (*Brandishing dagger.*) The end has come now, and by thy sacred wounds, O crucified mother, O Liberty, I swear that Russia shall be saved!

CURTAIN.

END OF ACT III.

ACT IV.

SCENE.—*Antechamber of the* CZAR'S *private room. Large window at the back, with drawn curtains over it.*

Present.—PRINCE PETROVITCH, BARON RAFF, MARQUIS DE POIVRARD, COUNT ROUVALOFF.

PRINCE PETRO. He is beginning well, this young Czar.

BARON RAFF (*shrugs his shoulders*). All young Czars do begin well.

COUNT R. And end badly.

1MARQ. DE POIV. Well, I have no right to complain. He has done me one good service, at any rate.

PRINCE PETRO. Cancelled your appointment to Archangel, I suppose?

MARQ. DE POIV. Yes; my head wouldn't have been safe there for an hour.1

(*Enter* GENERAL KOTEMKIN.)

BARON RAFF. Ah! General, any more news of our romantic Emperor?

GEN. KOTEMK. You are quite right to call him romantic, Baron; a week ago I found him amusing himself in a garret with a company of strolling players; to-day his whim is all the convicts in Siberia are to be recalled, and political prisoners, as he calls them, amnestied.

PRINCE PETRO. Political prisoners! Why, half of them are no better than common murderers!

COUNT R. And the other half much worse?

BARON RAFF. Oh, you wrong them, surely, Count. Wholesale trade has always been more respectable than retail.

COUNT R. But he is really too romantic. He objected yesterday to my having the monopoly of the salt tax. He said the people had a right to have cheap salt.

MARQ. DE POIV. Oh, that's nothing; but he actually disapproved of a State banquet every night because there is a famine in the Southern provinces. (*The young* CZAR *enters unobserved, and overhears the rest.*)

PRINCE PETRO. Quelle bétise! The more starvation there is among the people, the better. It teaches them self-denial, an excellent virtue, Baron, an excellent virtue.

BARON RAFF. I have often heard so; I have often heard so.

GEN. KOTEMK. He talked of a Parliament, too, in Russia, and said the people should have deputies to represent them.

BARON RAFF. As if there was not enough brawling in the streets already, but we must give the people a room to do it in. But, Messieurs, the worst is yet to come. He threatens a complete reform in the public service on the ground that the people are too heavily taxed.

MARQ. DE POIV. He can't be serious there. What is the use of the people except2 to get money out of? But talking of taxes, my dear Baron, you must really let me have forty thousand roubles to-morrow? my wife says she must have a new diamond bracelet.

COUNT R. (*aside to* BARON RAFF). Ah, to match the one Prince Paul gave her last week, I suppose.

PRINCE PETRO. I must have sixty thousand roubles at once, Baron. My son is overwhelmed with debts of honour which he can't pay.

BARON RAFF. What an excellent son to imitate his father so carefully!

GEN. KOTEMK. You are always getting money. I never get a single kopeck I have not got a right to. It's unbearable; it's ridiculous! My nephew is going to be married. I must get his dowry for him.

PRINCE PETRO. My dear General, your nephew must be a perfect Turk. He seems to get married three times a week regularly.

GEN. KOT. Well, he wants a dowry to console him.

COUNT R. I am sick of town. I want a house in the country.

MARQ. DE POIV. I am sick of the country. I want a house in town.

BARON RAFF. Mes amis, I am extremely sorry for you. It is out of the question.

PRINCE PETRO. But my son, Baron?

GEN. KOTEMK. But my nephew?

MARQ. DE POIV. But my house in town?

COUNT R. But my house in the country?

MARQ. DE POIV. But my wife's diamond bracelet?

BARON RAFF. Gentlemen, impossible! The old *regime* in Russia is dead; the funeral begins to-day.

COUNT R. Then I shall wait for the resurrection.

PRINCE PETRO. Yes, but, *en attendant*, what are we to do?

BARON RAFF. What have we always done in Russia when a Czar suggests reforms?—nothing. You forget we are diplomatists. Men of thought should have nothing to do with action. Reforms in Russia are very tragic, but they always end in a farce.

COUNT R. I wish Prince Paul were here. 3By the bye, I think this boy is rather ungrateful to him. If that clever old Prince had not proclaimed him Emperor at once without giving him time to think about it, he would have given up his crown, I believe, to the first cobbler he met in the street.

PRINCE PETRO. But do you think, Baron, that Prince Paul is really going?3

BARON RAFF. He is exiled.

PRINCE PETRO. Yes; but is he going?

BARON RAFF. I am sure of it; at least he told me he had sent two telegrams already to Paris about his dinner.

COUNT R. Ah! that settles the matter.

CZAR (*coming forward*). Prince Paul better send a third telegram and order (*counting them*) six extra places.

BARON RAFF. The devil!

CZAR. No, Baron, the Czar. Traitors! There would be no bad kings in the world if there were no bad ministers like you. It is men such as you who wreck mighty empires on the rock of their own greatness. Our mother, Russia, hath no need of such unnatural sons. You can make no atonement now; it is too late for that. The grave cannot give back your dead, nor the gibbet your martyrs, but I shall be more merciful to you. I give you your lives! That is the curse I would lay on you. But if there is a man of you found in Moscow by to-morrow night your heads will be off your shoulders.

BARON RAFF. You remind us wonderfully, Sire, of your Imperial father.

CZAR. I banish you all from Russia. Your estates are confiscated to the people. You may carry your titles with you. Reforms in Russia, Baron, always end in a farce. You will have a good opportunity, Prince Petrovitch, of practising self-denial, that excellent virtue! that excellent virtue! So, Baron, you think a Parliament in Russia would be merely a place for brawling. Well, I will see that the reports of each session are sent to you regularly.

BARON RAFF. Sire, you are adding another horror to exile.

CZAR. But you will have such time for literature now. You forget you are diplomatists. Men of thought should have nothing to do with action.

PRINCE PETRO. Sire, we did but jest.

CZAR. Then I banish you for your bad jokes. Bon voyage, Messieurs.4 If you value your lives you will catch the first train for Paris. (*Exeunt* MINISTERS.) Russia is well rid of such men as these. They are the jackals that follow in the lion's track. 5They have no courage themselves, except to pillage and rob.5 But for these men and for Prince Paul my father would have been a good king, would not have died so horribly as he did die. How strange it is, the most real parts of one's life always seem to be a dream! The council, the fearful law which was to kill the people, the arrest, the cry in the courtyard, the pistol-shot, my father's bloody hands, and then the crown! One can live for years sometimes, without living at all, and then all life comes crowding into a single hour. I had no time to think. Before my father's hideous shriek of death had died in my ears I found this crown on my head, the purple robe around me, and heard myself called a king. I would have given it up all then; it seemed nothing to me then; but now, can I give it up now? Well, Colonel, well? (*Enter* COLONEL OF THE GUARD.)

COLONEL. What password does your Imperial Majesty desire should be given to-night?

CZAR. Password?

COLONEL. 6For the cordon of6 guards, Sire, on night duty around the palace.

CZAR. You can dismiss them. I have no need of them. (*Exit* COLONEL.) (*Goes to the crown lying on the table.*) What subtle potency lies hidden in this gaudy bauble, the crown,7 that makes one feel like a god when one wears it? To hold in one's hand this little fiery coloured world, to reach out one's arm to earth's uttermost limit, to girdle the seas with one's hosts; this is to wear a crown! to wear a crown! The meanest serf in Russia who is loved is better crowned than I. How love outweighs the balance! How poor appears the widest empire of this golden world when matched with love! Pent up in this palace, with spies dogging every step, I have heard nothing of her; I have not seen her once since that fearful hour three days ago, when I found myself suddenly the Czar of this wide waste, Russia. Oh, could I see her for a moment; tell her now the secret of my life I have never dared utter before; tell her why I wear this crown, when I have sworn eternal war against all crowned men! There was a meeting to-night. I received my summons by an unknown hand; but how could I go? I who have broken my oath! who have broken my oath!

(*Enter* PAGE.)

PAGE. It is after eleven, Sire. Shall I take the first watch in your room to-night?

CZAR. Why should you watch me, boy? The stars are my best sentinels.

PAGE. It was your Imperial father's wish, Sire, never to be left alone while he slept.

CZAR. My father was troubled with bad dreams. Go, get to your bed, boy; it is nigh on midnight, and these late hours will spoil those red cheeks. (PAGE *tries to kiss his hand.*) Nay, nay; we have played together too often as children for that. Oh, to breathe the same air as her, and not to see her! the light seems to have gone from my life, the sun vanished from my day.

PAGE. Sire,—Alexis,—let me stay with8 you to-night! There is some danger over you; I feel there is.

CZAR. What should I fear? I have banished all my enemies from Russia. Set the brazier here, by me; it is very cold, and I would sit by it for a time. Go, boy, go; I have much to think about to-night. (*Goes to back of stage, draws aside curtain. View of Moscow by moonlight.*) The snow has fallen heavily since sunset. How white and cold my city looks under this pale moon! And yet, what hot and fiery hearts beat in this icy Russia, for all its frost and snow! Oh, to see her for a moment; to tell her all; to tell her why I am a king! But she does not doubt me; she said she would trust in me. Though I have broken my oath, she will have trust. It is very cold. Where is my cloak? I shall sleep for an hour. Then I have ordered my sledge, and, though I die for it, I shall see Vera to-night. Did I not bid thee go, boy? What! must I play the tyrant so soon? Go, go! I cannot live without seeing her. My horses will be here in an hour; one hour between me and love! How heavy this charcoal fire smells. (*Exit the* PAGE. *Lies down on a couch beside brazier.*)

(*Enter* VERA *in a black cloak.*)

VERA. Asleep! God, thou art good! Who shall deliver him from my hands now? 9This is he! The democrat who would make himself a king, the republican who hath worn a crown, the traitor who hath lied to us. Michael was right. He loved not the people. He loved me not.9 (*Bends over him.*) Oh, why should such deadly poison lie in such sweet lips? Was there not gold enough in his hair before, that he should tarnish it with this crown? But my day has come now; the day of the people, of liberty, has come! Your day, my brother, has come! Though I have strangled whatever nature is in me, I did not think it had been so easy to kill. One blow and it is over, and I can wash my hands in water afterwards, I can wash my hands afterwards. Come, I shall save Russia. I have sworn it. (*Raises dagger to strike.*)

CZAR (*staring up, seizes her by both hands*). Vera, you here! My dream was no dream at all. Why have you left me three days alone, when I most needed you? O God, you think I am a traitor, a liar, a king? I am, for love of you. Vera, it was for you I broke my oath and wear my father's crown. I would lay at your feet this mighty Russia, which you and I have loved so well; would give you this earth as a footstool! set this crown on your head. The people will love us. We will rule them by love, as a father rules his children. There shall be liberty in Russia for every man to think as his heart bids him; liberty for men to speak as they think. I have banished the wolves that preyed on us; I have brought back your brother from Siberia; I have opened the blackened jaws of the mine. The courier is already on his way; within a week Dmitri and all those with him will be back in their own land. The people shall be free—are free now—and you and I, Emperor and Empress of this mighty realm, will walk among them openly, in love. When they gave me this crown first, I would have flung it back to them, had it not been for you, Vera. O God! It is men's custom in Russia to bring gifts to those they love. I said, I will bring to the woman I love a people, an empire, a world! Vera, it is for you, for you alone, I kept this crown; for you alone I am a king. Oh, I have loved you better than my oath! Why will you not speak to me? You love me not! You love me not! You have come to warn me of some plot against my life. What is life worth to me without you? (CONSPIRATORS *murmur outside*.)

VERA. Oh, lost! lost! lost!

CZAR. Nay, you are safe here. It wants five hours still of dawn. To-morrow, I will lead you forth to the whole people—

VERA. To-morrow—!

CZAR. Will crown you with my own hands as Empress in that great cathedral which my fathers built.

VERA (*loosens her hands violently from him, and starts up*). I am a Nihilist! I cannot wear a crown!

CZAR (*falls at her feet*). I am no king now. I am only a boy who has loved you better than his honour, better than his oath. For love of the people I would have been a patriot. For love of you I have been a traitor. Let us go forth together, we will live amongst the common people. I am no king. I will toil for you like the peasant or the serf. Oh, love me a little too! (CONSPIRATORS *murmur outside*.)

VERA (*clutching dagger*). To strangle whatever nature is in me, neither to love nor to be loved, neither to pity nor—— Oh, I am a woman! God help me, I am a woman! O Alexis! I too have broken my oath; I am a traitor. I love. Oh, do not speak, do not speak—(*kisses his lips*)—the first, the last time. (*He clasps her in his arms; they sit on the couch together.*)

CZAR. I could die now.

VERA. What does death do in thy lips? Thy life, thy love are enemies of death. Speak not of death. Not yet, not yet.

CZAR. I know not why death came into my heart. Perchance the cup of life is filled too full of pleasure to endure. This is our wedding night.

VERA. Our wedding night!

CZAR. And if death came himself, methinks that I could kiss his pallid mouth, and suck sweet poison from it.

VERA. Our wedding night! Nay, nay. Death should not sit at the feast. There is no such thing as death.

CZAR. There shall not be for us. (CONSPIRATORS *murmur outside.*)

VERA. What is that? Did you not hear something?

CZAR. Only your voice, that fowler's note which lures my heart away like a poor bird upon the limed twig.

VERA. Methought that some one laughed.

CZAR. It was but the wind and rain; the night is full of storm. (CONSPIRATORS *murmur outside.*)

VERA. It should be so indeed. Oh, where are your guards? where are your guards?

CZAR. Where should they be but at home? I shall not live pent round by sword and steel. The love of a people is a king's best body-guard.

VERA. The love of a people!

CZAR. Sweet, you are safe here. Nothing can harm you here. O love, I knew you trusted me! You said you would have trust.

VERA. I have had trust. O love, the past seems but some dull grey dream from which our souls have wakened. This is life at last.

CZAR. Ay, life at last.

VERA. Our wedding night! Oh, let me drink my fill of love to-night! Nay, sweet, not yet, not yet. How still it is, and yet methinks the air is full of music. It is some nightingale who, wearying of the south, has come to sing in this bleak north to lovers such as we. It is the nightingale. Dost thou not hear it?

CZAR. Oh, sweet, mine ears are clogged to all sweet sounds save thine own voice, and mine eyes blinded to all sights but thee, else had I heard that nightingale, and seen the golden-vestured morning sun itself steal from its sombre east before its time for jealousy that thou art twice as fair.

VERA. Yet would that thou hadst heard the nightingale. Methinks that bird will never sing again.

CZAR. It is no nightingale. 'Tis love himself singing for very ecstasy of joy that thou art changed into his votaress. (*Clock begins striking twelve.*) Oh, listen, sweet, it is the lover's hour. Come, let us stand without, and hear the midnight answered from tower to tower over the wide white town. Our wedding night! What is that? What is that?

(*Loud murmurs of* CONSPIRATORS *in the street.*)

VERA (*breaks from him and rushes across the stage*). The wedding guests are here already! Ay, you shall have your sign! (*Stabs herself.*) You shall have your sign! (*Rushes to the window.*)
CZAR (*intercepts her by rushing between her and window, and snatches dagger out of her hand*). Vera!
VERA (*clinging to him*). Give me back the dagger! Give me back the dagger! There are men in the street who seek your life! Your guards have betrayed you! This bloody dagger is the signal that you are dead. (CONSPIRATORS *begin to shout below in the street.*) Oh, there is not a moment to be lost! Throw it out! Throw it out! Nothing can save me now; this dagger is poisoned! I feel death already in my heart.
CZAR (*holding dagger out of her reach*). Death is in my heart too; we shall die together.

VERA. Oh, love! love! love! be merciful to me! The wolves are hot upon you! you must live for liberty, for Russia, for me! Oh, you do not love me! You offered me an empire once! Give me this dagger now! Oh, you are cruel! My life for yours! What does it matter? (*Loud shouts in the street,* "VERA! VERA! *To the rescue! To the rescue!*")

CZAR. The bitterness of death is past for me.

VERA. Oh, they are breaking in below! See! The bloody man behind you! (CZAREVITCH *turns round for an instant.*) Ah! (VERA *snatches dagger and flings it out of window.*)

CONSPS. (*below*). Long live the people!

CZAR. What have you done?

VERA. I have saved Russia (*Dies.*)

TABLEAU.

Milton Keynes UK
Ingram Content Group UK Ltd.
UKHW032231011124
450424UK00008B/960